DEC 07 2015

GEMINI

Elizabeth Morgan

PowerKiDS press.

New York

Published in 2016 by The Rosen Publishing Group, Inc.
29 East 21st Street, New York, NY 10010

First Edition

Editor: Katie Kawa
Book Design: Katelyn Heinle

Photo Credits: Cover Yganko/Shutterstock.com; back cover, p. 1 nienora/Shutterstock.com; p. 5 Hong Li/Digital Vision Vectors/ Getty Images; p. 7 Babk Tafreshi/Science Source/Getty Images; p. 9 Andrey Lebedev/Shutterstock.com; p. 11 Apic/ Hulton Archive/Getty Images; p. 12 http://en.wikipedia.org/wiki/William_Herschel#mediaviewer/File:40_foot_telescope_ 120_cm_48_inch_reflecting_telescope_William_Herschel.png; p. 13 (William Herschel) Science & Society Picture Library/SSPL/ Getty Images; p. 13 (Uranus) Courtesy of NASA/JPL/STScI; p. 15 http://en.wikipedia.org/wiki/Eskimo_Nebula#mediaviewer/ File:Ngc2392.jpg; p. 16 © iStockphoto.com/inhauscreative; p. 17 John Chumack/Science Source/Getty Images; p. 19 http://en.wikipedia.org/wiki/Geminids#mediaviewer/File:Geminids.jpg; p. 21 © iStockphoto.com/knickohr; p. 22 Zack C/Shutterstock.com.

Library of Congress Cataloging-in-Publication Data

Morgan, Elizabeth, author.
 Gemini / Elizabeth Morgan.
     pages cm. — (The constellation collection)
 Includes bibliographical references and index.
 ISBN 978-1-4994-0932-1 (pbk.)
 ISBN 978-1-4994-0953-6 (6 pack)
 ISBN 978-1-4994-0985-7 (library binding)
 1. Constellations—Juvenile literature. 2. Constellations—Folklore—Juvenile literature. 3. Gemini (Constellation)—Juvenile literature. I. Title.
 QB46.M854 2016
 523.8—dc23
                                    2015006112

Manufactured in the United States of America

CPSIA Compliance Information: Batch #WS15PK: For Further Information contact Rosen Publishing, New York, New York at 1-800-237-9932

CONTENTS

TWINS IN THE SKY

Constellations are groups of stars that form the shapes of people, animals, or objects. One constellation looks like twin brothers standing together in the night sky. This constellation is Gemini, or the Twins.

Gemini was named after a Greek **myth** about twin brothers: Castor and Pollux. These are the names of the two brightest stars in this constellation, and they represent the heads of the twins. The basic shape of this constellation is a crooked rectangle. Lines of stars make up the rectangle's sides. Lines of stars also form the necks, arms, and legs of the twins, which branch out from the main rectangle.

THE RECTANGLE THAT MAKES UP THE MAIN PART OF GEMINI IS OFTEN SHOWN TO BE OPEN ON ONE SIDE. THIS IS THE SIDE OF THE CONSTELLATION THAT SHOWS THE TWINS' FEET.

CASTOR

POLLUX

STAR STORY
Some people believe Gemini shows Castor and Pollux holding hands or walking with their arms linked.

FINDING GEMINI

Gemini can be seen in the sky in both the Northern and the Southern **Hemispheres**. In the Northern Hemisphere, Gemini can be seen in the winter. In the Southern Hemisphere, Gemini is a summer constellation.

The easiest way to find Gemini is to look for Orion, which is another constellation. Orion, also known as the Hunter, can be spotted by looking for the line of three stars that make up the hunter's belt. If you look above Orion, you will be able to spot Gemini. Look for the stars Castor and Pollux, which are very bright and close to each other.

STAR STORY

Light pollution can make it difficult to see constellations, including Gemini. This kind of pollution occurs when man-made light gets in the way of natural light.

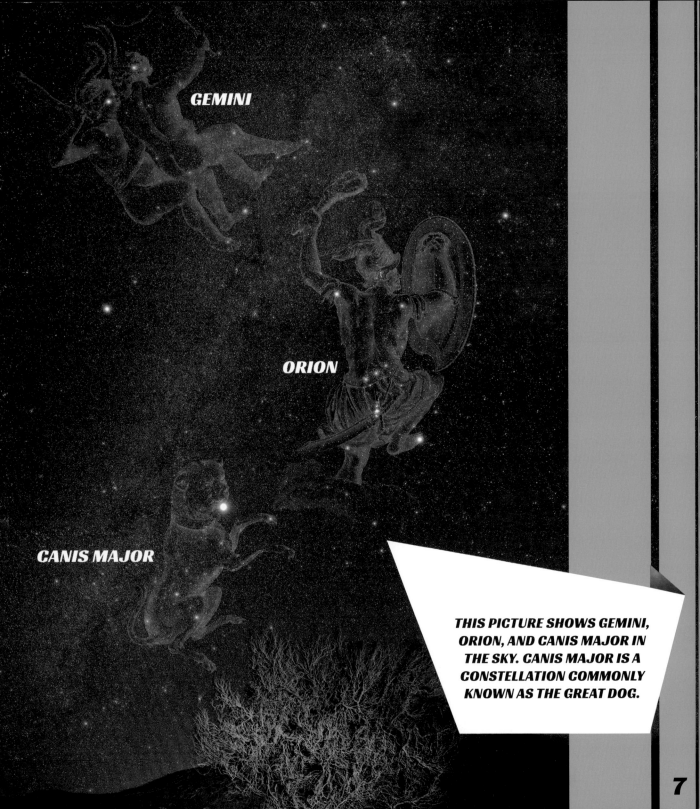

GEMINI

ORION

CANIS MAJOR

THIS PICTURE SHOWS GEMINI, ORION, AND CANIS MAJOR IN THE SKY. CANIS MAJOR IS A CONSTELLATION COMMONLY KNOWN AS THE GREAT DOG.

THE STORY OF THE TWINS

The ancient Greek myth of Castor and Pollux explained how these two brothers came to be seen in the sky. The twins' mother was Leda, the queen of Sparta. Each twin, however, had a different father. Castor's father was Leda's **mortal** husband. Pollux's father was Zeus, the king of the Greek gods. Because of who his father was, Pollux was immortal, which meant he couldn't die.

When Castor was killed, Pollux didn't want to live without him. He chose to share his immortality with his brother. Zeus then placed them together in heavens as the constellation known as Gemini.

STAR STORY

Other ancient cultures, including the ancient Romans, had their own versions of the myth of Castor and Pollux.

THE ANCIENT ROMANS BUILT A TEMPLE TO HONOR CASTOR AND POLLUX. THE PARTS OF THAT TEMPLE LEFT STANDING TODAY IN ROME, ITALY, ARE SHOWN HERE.

GEMINI IN THE ZODIAC

Gemini is also known as part of the zodiac. This is an imaginary band in the sky divided into 12 signs based on constellations. Many of the signs in the zodiac are animals. In fact, the word "zodiac" comes from a Greek phrase meaning "circle of animals."

Different constellations of the zodiac can be seen as Earth orbits, or moves around, the sun. Earth's orbit follows the circle of the zodiac. It may look like the constellations are moving, but it's actually Earth that's moving. The orbits of the moon and other planets lie within the circle of the zodiac, too.

STAR STORY
Different constellations of the zodiac are said to govern different periods of time. Gemini is believed to govern the time from around May 21 to around June 21.

PEOPLE ONCE USED THE ZODIAC TO MAKE MAPS, SUCH AS THIS ONE USED BY FRENCH SAILORS IN THE 1500S. GEMINI IS SHOWN ON THIS MAP AS A SET OF FEMALE TWINS.

A NEW PLANET

Astronomers have used constellations for thousands of years to locate and track important objects in the sky. Gemini helped discover a planet! William Herschel, a British astronomer, used a **telescope** he built himself to study the night sky. In 1781, he saw a point of light that

WILLIAM HERSCHEL'S TELESCOPE

moved through Gemini over time, which led him to believe that it wasn't a star. At first, he thought it was a **comet** because it was moving. However, it turned out to be the planet Uranus.

STAR STORY

Before Herschel discovered Uranus, astronomers only knew about the planets Mercury, Venus, Mars, Jupiter, and Saturn. Those planets can be seen with people's eyes.

Uranus was the first new planet to be discovered by astronomers using telescopes. Gemini played a big part in this important discovery.

URANUS

IN THIS PICTURE OF HERSCHEL, GEMINI CAN BE SEEN IN THE SKY BEHIND HIS HEAD.

WHAT'S A NEBULA?

Herschel also discovered a nebula that can be seen in the Gemini constellation. A nebula is a cloud of space dust and gas. In 1787, Herschel discovered the Eskimo Nebula in Gemini. This nebula got its name from the fact that it looks like someone wearing a furry hood.

The Eskimo Nebula is a planetary nebula. This kind of nebula is round like a planet. A planetary nebula is created when an old star dies. As its outer layers are blown away, clouds of dust and gas form. The Eskimo Nebula looks like a star with a blue-gray glow around it.

STAR STORY

The Eskimo Nebula is also called the Clownface Nebula because some people think it looks like a clown's face.

THE ESKIMO NEBULA ONLY LOOKS LIKE A BLURRY DOT IN GEMINI TO HUMAN EYES, BUT HIGH-POWERED TELESCOPES SUCH AS THE HUBBLE SPACE TELESCOPE ALLOW US TO SEE IT MORE CLEARLY.

CASTOR AND POLLUX

Astronomers study the bodies in space around and inside Gemini, but they also study the stars that make up the constellation. Pollux is the brightest star in Gemini, and it's 33.7 light-years from Earth.

STAR STORY
Castor and Pollux are light-years away from Earth. One light-year is equal to the **distance** light travels in one year, which is about 5.9 trillion miles (9.5 trillion km)!

Castor, which is 51.5 light-years from Earth, is actually more than just one star. It's a multiple star, which means it's a system, or group, made up of three or more stars. Castor is made up of six stars grouped into three pairs. The stars within a multiple star are bound together by gravity. Gravity is a force that pulls objects toward one another.

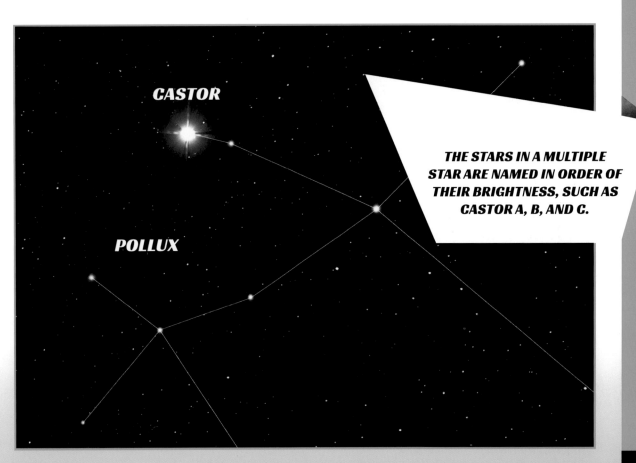

CASTOR

POLLUX

THE STARS IN A MULTIPLE STAR ARE NAMED IN ORDER OF THEIR BRIGHTNESS, SUCH AS CASTOR A, B, AND C.

THE GEMINIDS

Gemini is the place to look in the sky for a light show that happens every December. For around 10 days, it looks like shooting stars are falling from the constellation! These shooting stars are meteors, or pieces of rock or metal from space that burn up in Earth's **atmosphere** and create streaks of light in the sky. When many meteors appear at once, it's called a meteor shower.

The Geminid meteor shower can be seen by looking toward Gemini. At its peak, over 120 meteors can be seen per hour. These meteors are yellow and bright, which makes them easy to see.

MOST METEORS COME FROM COMETS, BUT GEMINIDS COME FROM AN ASTEROID. ASTEROIDS ARE SMALL, ROCKY BODIES THAT ORBIT THE SUN.

STUDYING STAR CLUSTERS

Gemini is home to a group of stars called an open star cluster. An open cluster is a group of stars that scientists believe came from the same nebula.

The open star cluster found in Gemini is called M35. The "M" comes from astronomer Charles Messier, who made a catalog, or list, of all the space objects he found before his death in 1817. This star cluster was the 35th object he found, so it was given the name M35. Astronomers think there are around 2,500 stars in M35. This cluster is believed to measure 30 light-years across.

STAR STORY
Scientists believe M35 is around 150 million years old, which is young for an object in space!

M35

THIS PHOTOGRAPH
SHOWS WHAT M35
LOOKS LIKE IN SPACE.

AN IMPORTANT CONSTELLATION

Gemini is a constellation that's been studied for thousands of years. Different groups of people throughout history came up with many stories to explain the twins in the sky. In modern times, astronomers from all over the world have looked closely at Gemini. The stars that make up the constellation and the space objects around and within it have given them many things to study!

If you go outside on a clear night, try to find Castor, Pollux, and the rest of the Gemini constellation. If you look in December, you may even see the Geminid meteor shower!

GLOSSARY

astronomer: A person who studies stars, planets, and other objects in outer space.

atmosphere: The gases that surround a planet or star.

comet: An object in outer space made mostly of ice and dust that often develops one or more long tails when near the sun.

distance: The space between two points.

hemisphere: Half of Earth.

mortal: Human and certain to die.

myth: A story told in ancient cultures to explain a practice, belief, or part of nature.

telescope: A tool used to see things that are far away.

INDEX

WEBSITES

Due to the changing nature of Internet links, PowerKids Press has developed an online list of websites related to the subject of this book. This site is updated regularly. Please use this link to access the list: www.powerkidslinks.com/tcc/gem